JAN 2 6 1996

Volleyball

the
SUMMER OLYMPICS

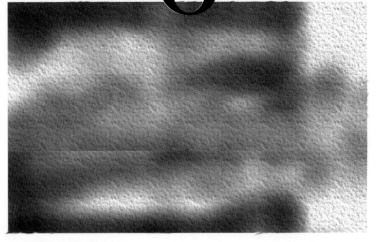

Volleyball

SUMMER OLYMPICS

PUBLISHED BY SMART APPLE MEDIA

Published by Smart Apple Media
123 South Broad Street, Mankato, Minnesota 56001

Cover Illustration by Eric Melhorn

Designed by Core Design

Photos by: Allsport, Bettmann Archives, Sports
Illustrated, Long Photography International and Wide
World Photos

Library of Congress Cataloging-in-Publication Data

Smale, David.
Volleyball/ by David Smale.
(The Summer Olympics)
Includes index.
Summary: Traces the history of volleyball as an
Olympic sport.

ISBN 1-887068-03-1

1. Volleyball—Juvenile literature. 2. Olympics—Juvenile
literature. [1. Volleyball—History. 2. Olympics.] I.
Title. II. Series.

GV1015.3.S62 1995   95-10458
796.325—dc20

HIGH-FLYING ACTION

High-flying, quick-striking action makes volleyball one of the most exciting of all sports. Crowds rise to their feet when they see a player soaring high above the net to smash the ball to the floor on the other side. Not surprisingly, volleyball is also one of the world's fastest-growing sports. It is played in more than 100 countries. In the United States, an estimated 65 million Americans take part in organized volleyball each year.

Setting it up for the kill.

Players leap high above the net to try to block the ball.

Invented in 1895, volleyball was originally considered an alternative for people who wanted an indoor sport that was less strenuous than basketball. Today, however, volleyball has evolved into a highly competitive sport that requires agility, quickness and power. There are six players to a side. The ball is put into play when one side serves it by hitting it over the net from behind the end line. The players then try to send the ball back over the net with three or fewer touches—and, if possible, to send it back over so the other team can't return it. Unlike many team sports, in volleyball points can be scored only by the offense. If the team receiving the serve wins the volley, it merely gains the serve. A team wins a game (or set) when it reaches 15 points with a margin of at least two points. The team that wins three out of five sets wins the match.

Though volleyball has long been popular in gymnasiums and on beaches, it is a relatively new sport on the Olympic landscape. It was added as a medal sport (for both men and women) in 1964. The next time the whole world gathers for intense volleyball competition, it will be at the centennial celebration of the Olympics in Atlanta in 1996. First-time winners Brazil (men) and Cuba (women) return to stake a claim at another gold medal, while perennial contenders Japan, the United States and teams from the former Soviet Union once again push for medal contention.

Volleyball requires split-second timing and teamwork (pages 10-11).

DRIVEN TO SUCCEED

Early Olympic women's volleyball competition was dominated by Japan and the Soviet Union. Both teams battled for the gold medal in each of the first four Olympics. At the 1964 Tokyo Games, the Japanese were favored to win—and not just because the tournament took place in their homeland. The Japanese women were coached by a hard-driving man named

Japan has always been a top power in women's volleyball.

Hirofumi Daimatsu. Daimatsu forced his players to train six hours a day, seven days a week, 51 weeks a year. During the practices, he verbally, psychologically and physically abused them. He also taught them many techniques new to the sport, such as the rolling receive, in which a player dives to the ground, hits the ball, rolls over and returns to her feet. His harsh but effective methods made the Japanese women the odds-on favorites to claim the gold. They cruised through the Games and only lost one set (to Poland) during the entire tournament—and that was when Daimatsu pulled his top players so that the Soviet coach could not see them play.

The final pitted the Japanese and the Soviets and drew an 80 percent audience share on Japanese television. After the

The Soviets (in black) smash a shot over the net.

Games, Daimatsu quit coaching. Four years later he was elected to the upper house of the Japanese Parliament. The Soviets won convincingly in 1968 and in a much closer contest in 1972. In the fourth set of the 1972 championship match, there were 24 service changes in a row (the team receiving the serve won the volley) without a point being scored. Finally, the Soviets managed to win a five-set match.

Perfect shots require total concentration.

Japan came back to claim the 1976 gold medal by dominating the competition even more than they did in 1964. Only one opponent (South Korea) reached double figures in scoring in one set, and the Japanese dispatched the Soviets 15-7, 15-8, 15-2 in the gold-medal game.

NEW CONTENDERS

Two straight large-scale boycotts in 1980 and 1984 disrupted the women's competition in volleyball. The Soviets won the gold on their home turf in 1980, when Japan was among the nations boycotting. In 1984, when the Soviets stayed home, Japan returned but won only the bronze.

The gold-medal fight was between two new contenders that year. The United States and China battled for the gold in a remarkable performance by the Chinese. Earlier, the two nations had competed in the preliminary rounds, with the United States taking the five-set match. But the Chinese came back in the gold-medal game and blitzed the U.S. 16-14, 15-3, 15-9.

Heading into the 1988 Seoul Games, which were not boycotted, China, the Soviet Union, Japan and Peru all had legitimate shots at the gold. Although Peru was new on the international scene, back home the team members were so famous they were simply known by their first names. The Peruvian women came back from a 14-9 deficit in the fifth set of the semifinal match against China to score seven straight points and claim a spot in the gold-

medal game. When the final match began at 6:30 a.m. Peru time, most of the country tuned in.

Peru stormed to a two-set lead in the final, but the Soviets reclaimed the momentum by winning the next two sets. The Soviets led 6-0 and 10-7 in the fifth set, only to have the Peruvians fight back to tie the score. Both teams survived match points before the Soviets won the final game 17-15.

Japan is set for the block.

In 1992 Cuba was the best team in the tournament, winning the gold-medal game without much difficulty over the Unified Team (composed of players from the former Soviet Union). The toughest competition for Cuba was against the American team in the semifinals. The two nations battled a grueling five-set struggle. In the fifth game, the score was tied seven times before the Cubans scored six of the last eight points to win the game and the match. The Americans went on to claim the bronze.

SOVIET MEN DOMINATE

Just as the Soviet and Japanese women dominated in the early days of Olympic volleyball, so have the Soviet men dominated their competition. The Soviet men have won a medal in every Olympic competition from 1964 to 1988. Their first gold medal was won in 1964 in Tokyo in a round-robin tournament. Czechoslovakia claimed the silver.

In 1968, the Soviets defeated Japan in four sets to claim their second gold medal. The only Soviet loss was to the United States in the first game. (Despite the early win, the U.S. team only mustered a seventh-place finish.) The Soviets claimed a bronze in 1972 in Munich and a silver in 1976 in Montreal before gaining their third gold in 1980 in Moscow. They didn't lose a match during the entire 1980 tournament.

Japan and Poland also put together strong teams in the 1970s. Japan, who won the bronze in 1964 and the silver in 1968,

came on strong in 1972 to take the gold medal. Four years later it was Poland's turn. The Polish men's national team won the 1976 gold medal largely because of intense physical training. The players used a unique training method that included jumping over a 4 1/2 foot barrier (1.37m) 392 times a day with 20- to 30-pound (9-14 kg) weights strapped on to their arms and legs.

In 1980, the Soviets reclaimed the gold medal in the boy-

The strategy is to catch an opponent out of position.

cotted Moscow Olympics. One of the teams that didn't partici-
pate that year was the American team, a team that was starting to
come into its own.

THE U.S. TAKES THE SERVE

Despite volleyball being an American-invented sport, the
American men were absent from medal competition in the early
Olympics. That changed in the 1980s when California began to
produce top-notch competitors. Players such as Karch Kiraly,
Dusty Dvorak, Ricci Luyties and Bob Ctvrtlik grew up in south-
ern California and honed their skills on the beaches of that re-
gion. Other players attended college in the area.

Entering the 1984 Olympics in Los Angeles, the United

Teamwork is the name of the game.

Facing Brazil at close range takes strength and courage.

States was hot. The team had won 24 straight matches, including four victories over the reigning world champion Soviets in Russia. But the Soviets boycotted the 1984 Games, so the United States' biggest competition came from Brazil. Although Brazil ended the American's winning streak with a straight-set victory in the preliminary rounds, the United States came back to overwhelm them in the gold-medal game. The Americans had won their first gold.

Four years later in Seoul, the U.S. men's team won its second gold. In the final round, the United States and the Soviet Union battled through two evenly matched sets with each team claiming one victory. Finally the United States wore down the Soviets and easily claimed the last two sets.

In the 1992 Barcelona Games, the biggest story was not the first-time champion Brazilians, or the Soviets, who failed for the first time to earn a medal in an Olympics in which they participated. Instead, the hairless Americans stole the show. Bob Samuelson, the emotional leader of the U.S. team, was penalized for yelling at the officials in a match against the Japanese. Samuelson's teammates felt the penalty was unjust. To show their support for their teammate, who was bald from a childhood disease, the rest of the U.S. players shaved their heads before their next match. They wore the chrome-dome look for the remainder of the competition, as well as on the medal stand, where they received the bronze.

Competition will be intense in Atlanta (pages 26-27).

When the Olympics arrive in Atlanta in 1996, the quest for the gold will continue. In the men's competition, the Brazilian team will face a tough challenge from the Americans, who want to reclaim the gold on their home court. The Netherlands men's team, which won the silver medal in 1992, should provide some tough competition as well.

In women's competition, Cuba will have to fight Brazil and Japan as well as the American women, who believe that the home-court advantage might be just enough to let them claim their first gold medal. And both men's and women's competition will be affected by the breakup of the Soviet Union.

Who will rise above the crowd to spike the competition? No one knows. But volleyball fans around the world are sure to enjoy the show.

Nothing compares with the excitement of victory (page 29).

volleyball

Men's Competition

Year	Gold	Silver	Bronze
1964	USSR	Czechoslovakia	Japan
1968	USSR	Japan	Czechoslovakia
1972	Japan	E. Germany	USSR
1976	Poland	USSR	Cuba
1980	USSR	Bulgaria	Romania
1984	USA	Brazil	Italy
1988	USA	USSR	Argentina
1992	Brazil	Netherlands	USA

Women's Competition

Year	Gold	Silver	Bronze
1964	Japan	USSR	Poland
1968	USSR	Japan	Poland
1972	USSR	Japan	N. Korea
1976	Japan	USSR	Korea
1980	USSR	E. Germany	Bulgaria
1984	China	USA	Japan
1988	USSR	Peru	China
1992	Cuba	Unified Team	USA